LIGHTNING BOOKS™

# Can You Tell a Cheetah from a Leopard?

**Buffy Silverman**

Lerner Publications Company

Minneapolis

To Jake,
who loves
cats

Lerner Publications Company
A division of Lerner Publishing Group, Inc.
241 First Avenue North
Minneapolis, MN 55401 U.S.A.

Website address: www.lernerbooks.com

Library of Congress Cataloging-in-Publication Data

Silverman, Buffy.
    Can you tell a cheetah from a leopard? / by Buffy Silverman.
    p.   cm. — (Lightning bolt books™—animal look-alikes)
    Includes index.
    ISBN 978-0-7613-6735-2 (lib. bdg. : alk. paper)
    1. Cheetah—Juvenile literature.  2. Leopard—Juvenile literature.  I. Title.
  QL737.C23S549  2012
    599.75'9—dc22                                              2010050813

Manufactured in the United States of America
1 — CG — 7/15/11

# Contents

# Built for Speed, Built for Power

Cheetahs and leopards look a lot alike. They are both large, spotted cats. Both are predators. They hunt other animals for food. Can you tell cheetahs and leopards apart?

Leopards (left) and cheetahs (right) look similar. Can you spot the differences?

Cheetahs are built for speed. They have long, skinny bodies. They can run as fast as a car drives on a highway!

A cheetah looks as if it can fly above the ground as it reaches top speed.

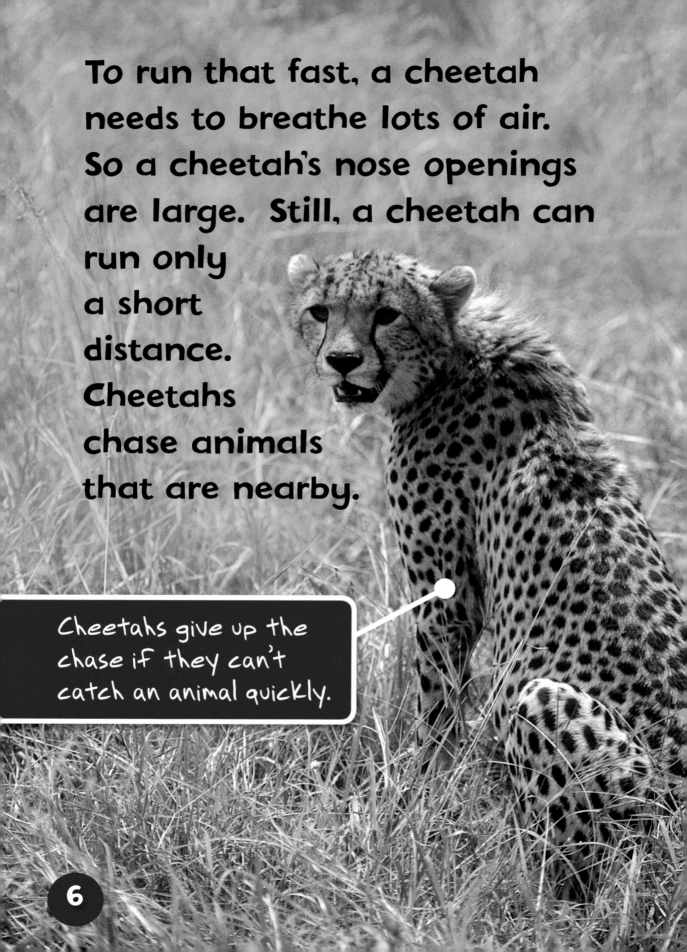

To run that fast, a cheetah needs to breathe lots of air. So a cheetah's nose openings are large. Still, a cheetah can run only a short distance. Cheetahs chase animals that are nearby.

Cheetahs give up the chase if they can't catch an animal quickly.

A cheetah races on long legs. In four strides, it leaps the length of a basketball court. A cheetah travels that far in one second.

This cheetah races across the grasslands in Africa.

Leopards are bigger
than cheetahs.

Their bodies are stronger.

And their paws are huge.

A leopard runs fast. But it can't run as fast as a cheetah. A leopard's legs are shorter than a cheetah's. Its body is heavier.

Leopards use their strength to catch a meal.  They sneak up on animals.  Then they pounce.

This leopard moves slowly through the tall grass.

A cheetah uses its tail to keep its balance.

A cheetah turns quickly to follow its prey. Prey are the animals a cheetah hunts. A cheetah's long tail helps it to balance. Its sharp claws and hard paws grip the ground.

Look at this cheetah's head. It looks small. A small head gives it a sleek shape like a race car.

Look at this leopard's large head. It has a strong, thick neck. A leopard's powerful jaw snaps shut on its prey.

Leopards are great climbers. Sharp claws grip tree trunks. Long tails help them to balance, just as cheetahs' tails do.

This leopard uses its sharp claws to climb a tree.

# Hide and Seek

Spots help animals to hide. Oval-shaped spots cover this cheetah's body. Its face has only a few spots. In tall grass, the cheetah seems to disappear.

Can you find the cheetah in this photo?

A leopard has spots on its body and its face. The spots are in groups. The groups form a rose shape. These spots let leopards hide in shady places. Sometimes leopards hide on leafy branches. They can drop from a tree to catch a meal.

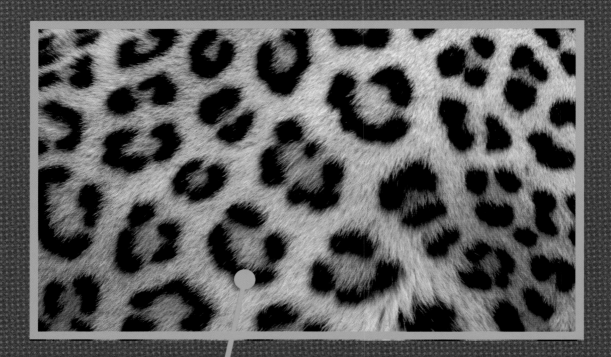

A leopard's coat has a beautiful spotted pattern.

Some leopards have black fur. Black leopards live in rain forests. There, trees grow close together. Sunlight does not reach the ground. Black fur makes leopards hard to see in rain forests.

This black leopard is hard to see in its dark forest home.

# Hunting Day and Night

Cheetahs hunt in daylight. Cheetahs have dark lines near their eyes. The lines stretch to the sides of the mouth. Dark lines act like sunglasses. The dark lines block bright sunlight. They help cheetahs to see.

These special markings help cheetahs see in the bright sun.

Leopards are nocturnal.
**Nocturnal animals hunt at night.** During the day, leopards usually rest in a tree.

A sleepy leopard naps in a tree during the day. It will hunt when night falls.

A leopard's huge eyes gather light. Light bounces off a special layer in its eyes. That helps the leopard to see in the dark.

This leopard's eyes look as though they glow in the dark.

# On the Prowl

A cheetah stands in tall grass. He looks down at the valley below. Sun shines on a group of gazelles. The cheetah watches. One gazelle wanders from the group.

This cheetah watches a nearby group of gazelles.

The cheetah sneaks closer.
Then he runs. The gazelle
speeds away. But the
cheetah runs faster.

This cheetah chases after
one gazelle from the group.
The others run to safety.

The cheetah knocks down his prey and bites its throat. He holds his prey while he catches his breath. Then he eats quickly. Other animals will try to steal his meal if he takes too long.

The cheetah's sharp teeth sink into the gazelle's neck.

Night falls. A leopard creeps through tall grass. A small herd of impalas is near. The impalas do not sense the leopard. But the leopard sees them. She watches and listens.

The leopard creeps closer. She does not make a sound. Suddenly the leopard pounces. She grabs an impala. She pulls it to the ground and bites its throat.

This leopard has caught its dinner.

The leopard drags her meal up a tree. Imagine carrying someone bigger than you up a tree. A leopard can do that! She hangs her food on a branch. No other animal will steal it.

A leopard is strong and graceful.

Cheetahs hunt in Africa's tall grasses.  Leopards prowl in the grasslands and forests of Asia and Africa.

Can you tell these look-alikes apart?

# Who Am I?

Look at the pictures below. Which are cheetahs? Which are leopards?

I have a long, skinny body.

I am big and strong.

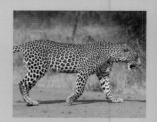

My head is large.

My head is small.

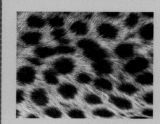

My spots are shaped like ovals.

My spots are grouped into rose shapes.

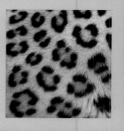

# Fun Facts

- Leopard cubs live with their mom. She teaches them to hunt. When they grow up, they live alone.

- When female cheetahs grow up, they stay near their mom. But they hunt alone. Males move far away. Brothers stay together for life and hunt as a group.

- Leopards hunt huge animals. But they also hunt mice and insects.

- Cheetahs hunt birds and rabbits. They hunt big animals too.

- Leopards also swim in lakes and rivers. They catch fish and crabs.

- Cheetahs are the fastest land animals in the world. They can run up to 70 miles (113 kilometers) per hour.

- Leopards live in many places. These include tropical forests, high mountains, grasslands, and deserts.

# Glossary

**claw:** a sharp, curved nail at the end of an animal's toes

**cub:** a baby cheetah or a baby leopard

**gazelle:** a small, graceful antelope

**impala:** a large, brownish antelope

**nocturnal:** active at night

**paw:** the foot of an animal with claws

**pounce:** to spring and grab prey

**predator:** an animal that hunts and eats other animals

**prey:** an animal that is hunted and eaten by other animals

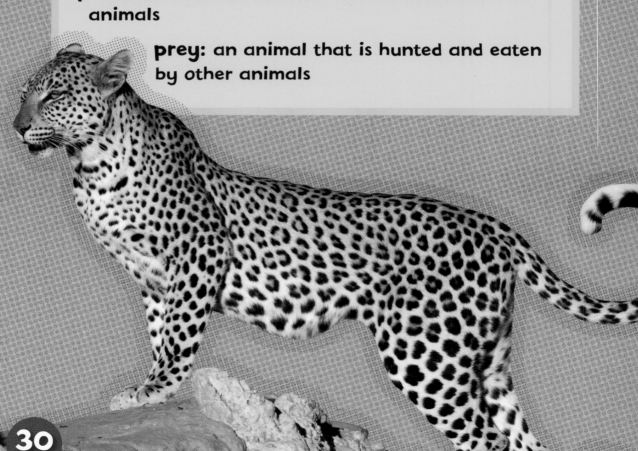

# Further Reading

Johns, Chris, and Elizabeth Carney. *Face to Face with Cheetahs.* Washington, DC: National Geographic, 2008.

Joubert, Beverly, and Dereck Joubert. *Face to Face with Leopards.* Washington, DC: National Geographic, 2009.

Levine, Michelle. *Speedy Cheetahs.* Minneapolis: Lerner Publications Company, 2007.

National Geographic Explorer: Leopard Lessons
http://magma.nationalgeographic.com/ngexplorer/pioneer/0704/articles/mainarticle.html

National Geographic Kids Creature Features: Cheetahs
http://kids.nationalgeographic.com/kids/animals/creaturefeature/cheetah

Patent, Dorothy Hinshaw. *Big Cats.* New York: Walker & Co., 2005.

# Index

# Photo Acknowledgments

The images in this book are used with the permission of: © age fotostock/SuperStock, pp. 1 (top), 7, 10, 27 (top); © Animals Animals/SuperStock, p. 1 (bottom); © Cusp/ SuperStock, p. 2; © Chrisbarton99/Dreamstime.com, p. 4 (left); © Gerry Lemmo, p. 4 (right); © G. Ronald Austing/Photo Researchers, Inc., pp. 5, 28 (top left); © James P. Rowan, pp. 6, 12, 18, 28 (middle right); © Hedrus/Dreamstime.com, pp. 8, 28 (top right); © Tom Brakefield/Stockbyte/Getty Images, pp. 9, 27 (bottom); © Martin Harvey/ Gallo/Getty Images, p. 11; © Ewan Chesser/Dreamstime.com, pp. 13, 28 (middle left); © Gerald Hinde/Gallo Images/Getty Images, p. 14; © Art Wolfe/Stone/Getty Images, pp. 15, 17; © Fritz Polking/Visuals Unlimited, Inc., pp. 16, 28 (bottom left & bottom right); © Karen Desjardin/Photographer's Choice/Getty Images, p. 19; © Mary Beth Angelo/Photo Researchers, Inc., p. 20; © Nomad/SuperStock, p. 21; © Adam Jones/The Image Bank/Getty Images, p. 22; © Anup Shah/Digital Vision/Getty Images, p. 23; © Tim Laman/National Geographic/Getty Images, p. 24; © Paula Coulter/naturepl. com, p. 25; © Kim Wolhuter/Gallo Images/Getty Images, p. 26; © Neal Cooper/ Dreamstime.com, p. 30; © Stock Connection/SuperStock, p. 31.

Front cover: © Francois6/Dreamstime.com (top); © Steffen Foerster/Dreamstime.com (bottom).

Main body text set in Johann Light 30/36.